9/2008   To my children
♡mommy

Let's Be Polite

P. K. Hallinan

ideals children's books.

Nashville, Tennessee

ISBN-13: 978-0-8249-5579-3

Published by Ideals Children's Books
An imprint of Ideals Publications
A Guideposts Company
535 Metroplex Drive, Suite 250
Nashville, Tennessee 37211
www.idealsbooks.com

Color separations by Precision Color Graphics, Franklin, Wisconsin
Printed and bound in Mexico by RR Donnelley

Library of Congress Cataloging-in-Publication Data

Hallinan, P.K.
  Let's be Polite / P.K. Hallinan.
     p. cm.
  Summary: Simple, rhyming verse presents many ways of being
polite and using good manners, such as not laughing when a playmate makes a mistake, always wiping one's feet before going inside,
and not interrupting when someone else is speaking.
  (alk. paper)
  [1. Etiquette--Fiction. 2. Manners and customs--Fiction. 3. Stories in
rhyme.] I. Title/

PZ8.3.H15Lch 2004
[E]--dc22
                                    2004003984

Designed by: Georgina Chidlow-Rucker

10 9 8 7 6 5 4 3 2 1

This book is for

_____

◆ ◆ ◆

From

_____

Being polite is the right way to be.
It blesses my friends

And my whole family!

When I need someone's help,
I like to say, "Please."

And then I say, "Thank you,"
For things I receive!

And when someone sneezes,
I'm certain to say,
"God bless you and keep you!"
Then be on my way.

Sometimes at supper, I long to be fed,
But I don't take a taste until grace has been said.

And always I'm careful, if I need to be heard,
To say, "Please, excuse me" and then share a word.

I keep my mouth closed while I'm trying to chew.

I stand to shake hands and say, "How do you do?"

And I try not to laugh
At a playmate's mistake,
When numbers of blunders
Are what we all make!

I wipe off my shoes as I cruise through the door,
'Cause that's why the mat's lying flat on the floor.

And I give up my chair so that others can rest—
Then friends feel like family, and family like guests!

And once in a while
I'll hurt someone's feelings,
But a simple "I'm sorry"
Starts any heart healing.

I don't interrupt someone trying to speak.

I don't ignore people who are feeble and weak.

Yes, I choose to use manners as the very best way
To honor the friendships that God sends my way.

So whenever I'm wondering which choices are right,
The handiest answer is . . .

Just be polite.